SPLINTERED

CROSSES

HALL POETRY COLLECTIVE

SPLINTERED CROSSES

SPLINTERED CROSSES

Copyright © 2015 **HALL POETRY COLLECTIVE**

All rights reserved. No part of this book may be reproduced or transmitted in any form or by any means, electronic or mechanical, including photocopying, recording, or by any information storage and retrieval system, without permission in writing from the publisher. All questions and/or request are to be submitted to: 134 Andrew Drive, Reidsville NC, 27320.

To the best of said publisher's knowledge, this is an original manuscript and is the sole property of the authors of **HALL POETRY COLLECTIVE** .

Printed in the United States of America

ISBN-13:978-0692453063
ISBN-10:0692453067

Printed by Createspace 2015
Published by BlaqRayn Publishing Plus 2015

Cover Design By: Jp Parson
Photograph Courtesy of : Johnathan Bass

Splintered Crosses

We, the authors, wish to dedicate our hard work and talent to someone special, You! You, the reader, are special! We want you to own that! We've composed this for you and many special people in our lives.

Our most gracious Heavenly Father reminds us continually how special we all are. He loves us always, no matter where we stand on our journey. With our words, we lift our hearts to glorify Him, honor Him, and offer gratitude for this wonderful life.

Our prayer is you will enjoy our selection of poems and perhaps find a few personal favorites.

God bless you abundantly,
*David Hall, Billy Charles Root, Angela Phipps and *Ron Hall*

Angela Phipps Black

Dedication:

To the One who walked
with me in my darkest hours,
Who has comforted me
when I was in tears,
the One who has loved me
beyond all measure,
my very ultimate treasure!
To the One who carried me
through the "valley of the shadow",
and has sustained me with His grace.
I love you, God.
　　　　　　　　–Angela

SPLINTERED CROSSES

PRODIGAL

Have you found yourself not worthy?
'Ever questioned, "What have I done?"
Have you found your life familiar
to that of the prodigal son?

Have you found yourself wallowing
in the slop of filth and much sin;
wishing you could go back in time;
start things fresh; all over again?

Have you found yourself with nothing,
empty, broken, and destitute?
... suffering the wages of your err?
... feeling you've total disrepute?

Run to our Father!
Run! Be swift! Don't tarry!

His face will beam with sheer delight!
His arms are waiting open wide!
It will be a celebration.
He's welcoming you. Go! Abide.

REBUILD ME

Tear me down!
Completely!
All the way down.

Search through all my rubble
for whatsoever's good;
then rebuild me, O Lord,
from Calvary's wood.

Make me strong and firm.
I don't wish to be grand.
Just rebuild me, Lord,
with your carpenter hands.

On Christ, the solid rock,
I'll forever stand.
Let me not be a fool
on sinking sand.

Tear me down!
Completely!
All the way down.

Sweep off the debris.
Make clean my foundation
(the very word of thee
given all creation.)

SPLINTERED CROSSES

Build me up.
Piece my peace.
Make me all new.

Let my hope be built
on Jesus' righteousness.
His blood washed the guilt
and I am beyond blessed!

On ' hill far away
stood an old rugged cross
that I may so say,
"I am found! I'm not lost!"

Use Calvary's wood!
Use carpenters hands!
Rebuild me, O Lord.

SPLINTERED CROSSES

Child for Today

Let me be just a child for today.
Skippity doo- -Skippity aye.
Let me catch sunbeams from the skies
and let them sparkle in my eyes!

Let me pick dandelions among the weeds
and I'll make wishes as I blow their seeds!
Let me blow bubbles and squeal with delight
as they float and drift and burst out of sight.

Let me be just a child for today.
Skippity doo --Skippity aye.
Let me run and jump and have my fun
all day long__ until day is done.

As the night draws near and I grow weary
take me in your arms, please, and carry me.
I will sigh a sigh of a child content,
for the whole day was wonderfully spent !

Help me find the rainbow _____ tomorrow .
(Zzzzz)

SPLINTERED CROSSES

Crumbling 'Neath Self Pity

On the cliff of self-pity
the rocks of "woes" and "Oh me"
crumbled easily beneath my feet
and I plunged in the pit of defeat.

In self-pity I wallowed
and despair there by followed.
Entrapped in my self-inflicted guile;
Scraped and bruised now lying in exile.

No desire for life remaining
Pleading to Death an end to bring-
The agony of a mind now defeated-
An empty aching heart uncompleted-

My heart it whispers its pain.
My mind quarrels such disdain.
Turmoil has diminished my value.
My soul in destitute needs rescue.

Out of clouding gloom, Peace appeared.
In the form of a dove it neared,
stirring courage from somewhere deep within
and strength, though small, sufficient to begin.

Dove of peace, perhaps a mirage,
my weakness remove and assuage.
Reaching and grasping, some hope visualized.
Hope of a good life, again realized.

SPLINTERED CROSSES

The MASTERpiece

I'm not a musician;
but, I have the most beautiful song!

I'm no preacher or politician;
but, I have a message
that to everyone belongs!

I'm not an artist.
I've not the skills to sculpt
or design;
but, I have a MASTERpiece
in my heart,
my soul,
and my mind!

If I could . . .
I'd sing sweetly.
I'd sing loud and strong!
I'd give voice to this love;
this love above all others;
so wondrous,
so divine!
Oh, ___ I'm so very wealthy
because it is mine!

It was carved!
It is whittled!
It is huge!
It is real!

SPLINTERED CROSSES

Open your eyes!
Behold Calvary's hill!

Look at love's exhibit.
Listen to the words.
There's no denying the grandeur!
Completely Awesome ___Breathtaking Love___
displayed__ for everyone.

SPLINTERED CROSSES

The Willow Danced

The willow tree danced beside us.
The Tennessee sky was always blue.
My memories are only happy
Of those summer times spent with you!

Side by side for hours we would swing;
Laughing 'til it hurt and singing tunes;
Snapping green beans and shelling purple hulls .
Nights always came a bit too soon.

Fresh fruits and homegrown garden picks
Made dinner time a more special meal.
After all, I had hoed weeds, turned the soil,
Watered, picked, shucked, snapped, helped, and peeled.

We traipsed through the Smoky Mountains.
You showed me the beauty in nature.
We roasted marshmallows over fire.
'Tired from all our adventures.

The Willow dances in my mind
Bringing back all these fun memories
Of an aunt who made me feel special
And to her niece, she'll always be!!!
~

SPLINTERED CROSSES

What's In Your closet?

Worn shoes that walk
in yesterdays?
garments soiled and stained
from by gone mistakes?
Tucked away treasures
of little value?

What's in your closet?

The truth smothered 'neath
deceit and foul lies
in all the corners?
slippery satin
secrets you must keep
til your end of days?

What's in your closet?

Open painful wounds
you will not let heal?
You swaddle 'em close.
bleeding unforgiveness?
shelves of bitterness
weighted heavily?

What's in your closet?

Negativity
hung on bent hangers?

SPLINTERED CROSSES

blankets of lost hopes?
attitude clutter
of bad opinions
taking up much space?

What's in your closet?
mind?
heart?
spirit?

LEAVES

leave the Womb
leave Childhood
leave School
leave the Nest . . .
The Collection grows
larger through seasons.

leave fallen Unforgiveness,
leave brittle Bitterness,
leave dry shriveled Dead Promises. . . gather
together
dispose or burn Them.

Don't leave
golden Dreams,
Peaceful greens,
burning red Loves.
Enjoy them hanging
on to your tree of
life.

With the next strong wind
they might withstand.
They might fall,
dance on a breeze,
or
drift from sight
and be Leaves.

SPLINTERED CROSSES

WHEN I COME

When I come to Thee
With heartache and tears...
When I come,
You offer comfort.

When I come to Thee
Feeling lost, confused...
When I come
You direct my way.

When I come to Thee
With my heavy load...
When I come
You quite gently lift.

When I come to Thee
Questioning this life...
When I come
You give me answers.

When I come to Thee
Swallowed in darkness...
When I come
You shed light on me.

When I come to Thee
Needing to be loved...
When I come
You love me. You love!

SPLINTERED CROSSES

When I come to Thee
You are there waiting
With wide open arms.
You wrap your sweet love
Around me tenderly.
You raise and set me
On Your higher plain.
You always, always,
Without conditions
Love me completely!

SPLINTERED CROSSES

I Like Country

Country roads grumble 'neath
crunching tires on gravel.
Country sunshine is bright,
unrented by buildings.
Country music is picked
and strummed with guitar thumbs.

Country life welcomes you
as do the people, too,
sitting on their porches
waving as you drive by.
Unlike in the city
horns are a "hello"
a "nice to see you, too".

There's fields of straight rowed crop
divided by rich dirt.
The blue sky's wide open.
Treetops stretch way up high.
The breeze blows fresh and sweet
often with home cooking
announcing, "time to eat."
A holler can be heard
clear down around the bend.

At night the stars come out.
They dance and twinkle bright.
The volume of the day
becomes an easy lull.

SPLINTERED CROSSES

While locust sing in trees
the critters start to sneak.
Country life ends early
when day is all but done.

Country folk know just how
to relax and take it easy
and have some country fun.

SPLINTERED CROSSES

I ONCE WAS LOST; BUT, NOW I AM FOUND
- Acrostic

Immensely impaired

Out of my mind
Neurotic and numb
Casualty of corruption
Encumbered by emptiness

Weary and weak
Afflicted with anguish
Stricken by sorrow

Lying in loneliness
Out of my mind
Sprained on sadness
Tortured by troubles

BUT NOW,

Improvement is implicit

Acceptance has arrived
Mercy is magnificent

Freed from fear
Opportunity has opened
Understanding unrelinquished
Newness is nourished
Determination declared!

SPLINTERED CROSSES

DECEIVED

Appearing as harmless sheep
deceiving and misleading
to paths of damnation.
Because of their trickery
many have been caused to err.

They transformed themSELVES.
They are false profits
teaching false doctrines.

They've perverted His gospel;
substituting with fables
purposed to serve their passion.
They have turned away from truth
and lifted theirSELVES up high.

God is not the author
of such confusion
but, of truth and peace.

People are being taught in part.
Thus, they have learned only in part.
God knows who are His believers.
Test the spirits. Look at the fruits
that you might know 'who are His', too.

Do not be deceived.
On the judgment day,
Some will hear "depart".

SPLINTERED CROSSES

FREEDOM

Freedom is straight.
When you look left,
when you look right,
it is forward.

Freedom lights the way.
It is not shadowed.
It is before us
guiding and bidding.

Freedom moves in stillness.
It maps the distance
giving sound direction
making steadfast ways.

Freedom speaks in the silence;
counseling the heart and soul,
beckoning with tenderness;
sweetly giving instruction.

Freedom awaits to be welcomed
into your heart, into your being.
Freedom is always within reach.
Freedom comes in The Way, The Truth
and Light!

MEALTIME

My aunt's kitchen was joyful like
her.
Preparing meals was a fun activity.

Fresh vegetables from the garden
wafted fragrances from stove pots
steaming.
Bright red and orange tomatoes sliced
thick
decorating charming serving
platters.
White creamy butter pats ready for
use.
Fresh brewed tea poured over ice cubes
in mason jars.
Rolls dripping in butter will melt in
mouths.
White napkins placed by each plate
setting.

Following our thanks for the bounty
provided.
Indulging in all of our favorite garden
foods.
Telling stories, sharing laughter,
filling stomachs,
enjoying the full experience of meal
time.

SPLINTERED CROSSES

Peace of Mind

The air is crisp.
The morning new.
The day has hope.
My worries' few!

I don my clothes
and splash my face.
The day ahead
I will embrace.

'Grab my jacket.
I'm out the door
... daylight stillness
off to explore.

My ears they find
the pigeons coo,
a whistling train,
and stillness, too.

My eyes scope out
the new dawn sky,
deserted streets,
trees reaching high.

In exploration
the present I find.
life is discovering
my own peace of mind!

I AM

I am southern Baptist.
I am Roman Catholic.
I am united Methodist.
I am Presbyterian.
I am a church goer?

I am Christian.
I am a Jew.
I am Hindu.
I am Muslim.
I am this labeled faith?

WE ARE children of God!
Made in His own image!
We're brothers and sisters!
One, big- -huge family
(Well we're supposed to be)!

I am Nothing.
I AM is everything!

"Thy kingdom come.
Thy will be done..."

When the world
allows HIM
to govern
HIS kingdom
in our hearts

SPLINTERED CROSSES

there will be
Peace on earth!
When HIS kingdom
comes in me
I'll know peace.
When HIS kingdom
comes in you,
You'll know peace.
When HIS kingdom
comes in us
You and I
will share peace!

SPLINTERED CROSSES

RETURN TO LOVE

Fallen from grace,
return to love!
Fall on your face!

Standing in the synagogues,
in Mosque on the floor,
and bowing at altars, but
love not any more.

Jews, Christians, Muslims - alike
claiming they know God;
but hating one another.
their hearts are so fraud.

Followers or Believers?
which? __ what believe you?
Do your daily life actions
reflect His word, too?

Children of God, we ALL are!
We've ALL fallen from grace.
Let us ALL, you, me, and them,
fall before HIM on our face...
And return to LOVE.

THE ANSWER

People often question

The true meaning of love
especially at times
when all they can think of
is their heart's beat don't rhyme.

It seems that love has failed
to be as they believed.
The love they imparted
is wounded and not received.

The love of their life departed
leaving them hurting and without.
They have questions and confusion.
Existence of love they doubt.

God will give the answer.

Look to our Father up above.
He will dry our every tear
and teach us the meaning of love.
He is waiting to draw us near.

Call on Him. Follow in His way
and the love in your heart will grow
and multiply stronger day by day.
The meaning of love you will know.

SPLINTERED CROSSES

TO EVERYTHING THERE IS A SEASON

Parental heart's cry joy
at birth's arrival.
Labor pains vanish
instantaneously .
{a time to be born}
{and a time to die.}

Sorrowing hearts cry
immense wrenching pain
at loss of precious
lives they held so dear.
{A time to weep}

Unsuspectingly a smile
spreads those tears stained cheeks.
Someone is laughing.
Much to your surprise __it's you.
{A time to laugh}

The tears are much fewer.
Self-control has strengthened.
The pain is still present;
but, you manage it well.
{A time to mourn}

One day you notice
the sun is brighter.
The breeze is gentle
and it's touching __you.

SPLINTERED CROSSES

You hear a bird tweeting.
It's been a long time.
A strange freedom inside
starts dancing in you.
{A time to dance}

You contemplate this life.
Perhaps it can be good.
You consider loving
yourself __ once again.
{A time to love}

SPLINTERED CROSSES

WITHIN REACH

It is my learned conclusion,
the author of confusion
is constantly writing
thoughts that cause dividing.

Facts get shoved aside
by doubt-birthed made- up lies
and the things truly real
are smothered by a "feel".

Confusion brews in a pot
and whistles things that are not.
Despair chokes out the breath
from hopes and dreams abreast.

Coals of utter defeat
smolder near at your feet.
One flash fire can consume.
Aspirations, then seem doomed.

When all the while. . .

Just within your reach
is the truth you should beseech.
Look, Listen, and obey
to the maker of your day.

What Does LOVE Start With?

C?
Child's play time with range of Colors
Creating art for their parents
Custom made with haphazard Care

M?
Mother singing sweet Melodies
Multitasking with Merriment,
Maintaining all for household

K?
Knuckles, that now resemble Knobs,
Kneading dough into homemade bread,
Knowing her loved ones will delight.

F?
Father working daily to Feed
Family and provide their needs
Fully committed to loving.

S?
Son giving life a Sacrifice
Salvation from a world of sin.
Son of God, Jesus Christ Savior

IT IS

A silent gratitude upon awakening
"Aah, the birds are chirping!"

A longing desire of the heart
connecting with a lonesome train whistle

A thankfulness for the warm water
showering over your skin and hair

The delight of smelling bacon as it wafts
from the breakfast skillet through the air

The stillness of your being bowed
before the presence of Him in morning worship

The plea of "Help" in the daily commute
of congested traffic and reckless drivers

The satisfaction of warm fresh coffee
to jump start the day of demands and deadlines

The muttered request for a quick guidance
to resolve complications that suddenly arise

It is a smile with which you greet a stranger
just to share the compassion of your heart

A sigh of relief in a checkout stand
with reason, the total did not exceed your limit

The earnestness of your heart
to present your best self to your family and friends

It is a tear quickly brushed away
to not be seen or questioned.

The thanksgiving you offer at mealtime
for food, bounty, and blessings in your life

The expression of contentment
as you survey your surroundings or circumstances.

Your heart, mind, and soul raised humbly
before the Almighty God, our Father, our Creator

It is prayer.

Ron Hall

SPLINTERED CROSSES

Wonders and Joys

What wonders we do behold
Foraging through the Bible of old
Reading the stories to be retold
Time tested and tried as pure gold

Tis God who lifts man from sand
To a foundation, solid and grand
Tis His love for frail and mortal man
To a place secure in His eternal hand

O wretched man, I shall ever be
Without the presence of the Son of Eternity
Darkness befalls me in troubled seas
My voice I lift from bended knees

What joy besets me when His voice I hear?
My heart is yielded in desires so clear
The matchless Wonder stands so near
To wipe away the smallest tear

Bound by Nails

Onward He trod, up the hill, blood dripping from His head to His heel.
Weakened by the cross, forsaken by all, oh what agony he must feel.
Finally to the top, He came to stop; the old rugged cross laid on the ground.
There He stepped forward as His body by three Roman nails was bound.

Not a word, maybe a sigh, He laid himself upon the cross to die.
A broken brokenhearted mother in horror bound sent forth her languishing cry.
"Son, behold thy mother" to John He spoke, "Woman behold thy son".
Keep thy bond together, I shall return for the battle is already won.

On many foreign and distant hills, men have given their life on the battle field.
Men and women to this day stand, the Faith they proclaim their only shield.
Come my friend let not the royal banner of Christ fall silent to the ground.
For there beside Him stands the heavenly host waiting for the trump to sound.

Across Jordan to the Promise Land

There is a river that is called Jordan
They say that it is deep and it is wide
Tis thru Jesus the Son, the Savior
Hope is given to reach the other side

All my life has been given to Jesus
Upon His glorious word I gladly stand
Precious promises carry my languishing soul
To rest forevermore in Heaven's Promised Land

Oh, river of chilling waters to cross one day
Will you, as long ago, divide for me once more?
For from this earthly shore, my soul must take
It's journey to Jordan's peaceful shore

Into the flowing waters of Jordan I leap
Yes my eyes are open, the land I see
My soul was given unto thee forever to keep
It is, and forever shall be, my place to be

SPLINTERED CROSSES

Tear Stained Words

If anyone should inquire of me
Of the one place most desirable to see
Why without hesitation, I would respond
To the land of lost souls and fields beyond

Golden fields of harvest in reach of mortal man
Empowered laborer is part of His eternal plan
Upon bended knees and tear stained cheeks
The weeping heart His will doth seek.

Master Divine thy tender voice is gladly heard
From the brightened pages of thy Holy Word
Tears doth encircle words of fine print
To reach the lost at any cost is what Jesus meant

In or Out

Open door
Floral beauty
Silent stand
People turn

Hearts break
Eyes water
Tears flow
Shoulders shake

Lips quiver
Words hollow
Arms squeeze
Knees buckle

Hands restless
Emotions rattle
Backs weaken
Coffin closes

Reconcile

Listen to me, my little child
While I tell of a love worthwhile
The reaching down to reconcile
Sinful man who has gone his last mile

Who shall go to earth to pay?
The sinner's debt and show the way
None but Jesus stepped forward that day
Let me go, let them hear what I have to say

It shall be to them a total surprise
For in a stable and manger I shall lie
Angelic voices singing from on high
Shepherds rejoicing, glory filling their eyes

The Burden to Share

Who should now step thru heaven's portal gates?
But the Son of the Highest, for man's place to take.
None but the Only Begotten Son, the Holy one could purify.
For without the shedding of His blood man would die.

His goal was simple, for the soul of mankind he would vie.
To the cross of Calvary, he would pay for every sin and lie.
The weight of the cross was too heavy alone to bear.
One was called alongside the burden to share.

From the crowd Simon the Cyrenian was forced to kneel.
To lift the wooden cross from the One so genteel.
For him the heavy cross was not so difficult to bear.
For he could see at the end a crown he would surely wear.

Billy Charles Root

I dedicate these selected poems
first and foremost to my Lord and Savior Jesus Christ,
for he has given me the ability to write.
Secondly I dedicate the same poems to my family
who always stand by me and encourage me to continue on
when nobody reads my work.
And last but not least I dedicate these poems
to my country and countrymen,
may we never forget what makes us great
and that it is founded on Christ and in family amen.

SPLINTERED CROSSES

American Roots

Faded stop signs
Cracked blacktop roads
Busted Chevy in every yard

Rib-it song played by toads
Gone fishin with cane poles
Saturday afternoon playin cards

Drinkin from the hose
That's just the way it goes
All the grownups still get outside

Play with all the kids
Even when life hits the skids
Some seek while the others hide

Simple livin
Simply done
Out here in the sticks

Cookin meat
You never thought you would eat
Gotta love them hicks

Church bells toll every Sunday morn
The whole town knows your name

Everyone stops by for a visit
And they all think the city is lame

Small town USA
Where Time still stands still
This is from where we came
And we always will

SPLINTERED CROSSES

Come to the Table

Come to the table, let us all gather round
Let us sit and partake, of the joy we've found
We'll pass the bread and the cup filled to the brim
Together let us rejoice in his covering of our sin

We will speak of the cross and how it filled this cup
And how the bread was torn so we could eat it up
Let our memory recall the savior's gentle voice
When he told each of us, we were his hearts choice

Come with me, to the upper room
Let us sit and eat with the bridegroom
Let the breaking of bread now commence
Until the full of this night is fully spent

Let us do this often that we remember and not forget
The love that knew no height nor depth
And if we lose our place along this path of life
Just look for the window and the upper room light

Demon's Breath

Demon's breath
upon my neck
the sin within caress

Rebirthing memory
of yestergone days
Reflections of the wretch

Festering gaze
of evil ways
how I was back when

Refreshing the deeds
the growth of demon seeds
pig in the mire splashing around in sin

Tongue flicker against my lobe
dead man plans glittery strobe
my ear begins to itch

Sound of desire
lustful fire
unwanted but still I twitch

A loss of me
is all I see
demons laugh in my ear

Mind on fire

brow perspire
drown within my fear

Dark no sight
soul in plight
see a candle burn

Stare full forward
eyes on flame and word
slowly I turn

Translucent patterns of thought and time
wash out the dirty feet of my mind
now I see you for what you truly are
now I reach for the bright morning star

Come to my rescue
take me away
nothing more the demon can say

With shivers he leaves me
into the shadows he goes
the light now with me
I fear no more foes

SPLINTERED CROSSES

10 Years.

Ten years ago you killed me
To get what you wanted
I was discarded
Who I was died
Marriage fried
When you tore the boys from me
Like a scab
Oh yeah
My bad
I mean fell out of love with me
You wanted to be free
On the floor you left me in a death bleed
Not even a hankie
To coagulate
The flow
While I slowly died slow
It was your show
So I had to learn to walk again
Stand up again
And become different than other men
You dropped me
But father God caught me
And taught me
For this journey of longevity
Learning to forgive you
And me
And at the beginning
When I was most hurting
He sent me to her

My rock shoulder
For crying
And she held me while I cried over you
Who does that
Loving someone and holding them
As they fall out of it with another
She is my eighth wonder
And life has been a hell I couldn't dream up
Tall and bitter cup
I've endured a transformation
Through lamentation
And a new configuration
While you built tinker bells
Fairy tale
And what?
You thought a happily ever after
A book of dreams with endless chapters
Would never ask you to face truths answers
But now you have no choice
Times, they are a changing
And the seeds you planted are rearranging
And you're upset cause now you get to eat the fruit
Unwisely spent loot
You know what they say about life
Reap what you sow
Keep what you kill
I'm sorry it is this way
But it is, still
I wish you no harm or curse
Dumped on the floor, life's purse
Or a ride in the hearse

SPLINTERED CROSSES

But I wonder if you look at them like I do
What have you taught them that is truth
When your cross is heavy, you lay it down
Drop it like it's hot
On the dirty ground
And now wonder why they're dropping you
Seriously, what did you expect they would do
I wish you would take a look
At the writing of your own book
Or better yet at His
I've hung a wreath upon my door
Don't love you anymore
Only them
The lost parts of me
And her
Who puts up with who you forced me to be
And Him
Who has never been gone from my side
I know he loves you too
But unto him have you cried?

SPLINTERED CROSSES

The Baptizer

I am the unbarrened child of Elizabeth
And son of Zacharias
A Nazarite that dwelleth
By way of the wilderness

I primed the ears and hearts of the people
For the arrival of his highness
My voice cried out in wilderness steeples
Calling for baptism and repentance

And then he came
The glorious splendor of true light
Now with nowhere to hide
He illuminated souls deceived in dark lies

As his light grew bright
My voice willingly faded quiet
As my time trickled down
I was locked away, prison bound

I had confronted Herod the king
Of this unlawful adulterous thing
Herodias his bride was his brother's wife
My conviction brought their lies to light

When Herod wanted his bride's daughter
He promised her all that he could offer
Her and her mother devised a plan
To get rid of me by the kings hand

SPLINTERED CROSSES

Bring me the dippers head
Baptizer John, I want him dead
On a platter bring me his scull
Do it at once, do it now, go

Herod being a man of his word
Became grieved and deeply disturbed
Lust was more important than his soul
For lust confronted, my head would roll

Thus marked the beginning anew
First to die for light with light now in view
Beheaded for truth better than alive in lies
But this was only my earthly demise

SPLINTERED CROSSES

Skyline

The Oklahoma City skyline emerges from the night
Peach clouds dot the morning sky
In the distance City lights seem like fireflies
I'm cruzin Interstate forty in something we call a dinosaur

And as the sky evolves into a fire glow in this morning's sunrise
The dingy city sparkles with warmth for a short spell
Before it becomes covered in its people like ants In a colony

My how far you have come little city
Once an undesirable location or destination
Now a river walk and fancy downtown district
Complete with overpriced parking
And over budgeted construction

And as the hues of the morning fade
into the distance the cement tones come forth
The panhandlers all take their places
And the executives all zip along
In cars not made in countries that they make their wealth in

The hood areas start hoping with activity

as the poor make their ways to crappy jobs and day care drop offs
The health department and human services offices already have lines forming outside their doors

The hopeless homeless awake from their cardboard tents
and newspaper covers and begin another day of thinking and crying

Though there are churches with open doors for the needy
Most are practicing their Sunday songs and cleaning the sanctuaries
And the needy, well they walk right on by, unnoticed.

As I enter the one year ago tornado ravaged areas
I find the human spirit and resilience
have transformed the war zone
into clean real estate and rebuilt civilization once again

And the cities breathe and life continues.
In fact we almost seem bored and robotic.

SPLINTERED CROSSES

Roadside Memorial

A cascade of days and one lane driving
Yellow and white lines in the center dividing
Straight ahead vision, watch where you're going
Traffic ahead of me begins slowing
Two lane highway, destination unreached
Unknown reason, traffic flow breached
Squeaky stop and I look around
Side of the road cross perception found
A makeshift memorial on the other side of the road
Memories of a loved one, now there abode
I wonder what happen, what caused the memories to stop there
So many busy travelers pass by without care
Was it a violent catastrophe the loud noises of life's end
With the demons the cause and did angels descend
I suppose we'll never know what did their unfold
The purpose of that memorial on the other side of the road

Impoverished

Poverty oh poverty why dost thou oh bother me
Is it the color of my skin that you seek
Or the language of my land in which I speak
Maybe the salt from the tears that i weep

Three jobs I work and my mate ran away
It takes all I've got to put some food on a plate
Social services says I make too much for help
Meanwhile nothin but beans on a fallen down shelve

I'm beggen for scraps off richly fat tables
They count their money's in my face
And as they laugh gleefullly their bellies unstable
I can't help but wonder, is my life a waste?

It's like wearing cement shoes walkin round hungry
Workin to pay tax on help I can't get
Special needs minimum wage so dang ugly
While I avoid the landlord, I owe two months rent

With nothing left they took the kids
Life on the street isn't fit they said
No reason left to live this impoverished life
No longer a father, or husband
No longer mother nor wife

No strength left to fight this fight

SPLINTERED CROSSES

They lose themselves in the dark of night
Dreaming of how to make things light
Hoping their babies are all alright

The hands of the Devils shackling ankles
They hold down most but, every once in awhile
Some bust loose and they grab the cross
They pick themselves up
and dust themselves off

With a tiny little spark
They light like a torch
That stands at the opening
Of King Jesus court's

They light the way
With the flame of grace
Back where they started
They light others flames.

The poor useth entreaties;
but the rich answereth roughly

SPLINTERED CROSSES

One Grain.

The weary day's eyes fall heavy
At the closing of the sunlight limit
Slow blending of the day and the night
And this side of the earth drifts into slumber
Yielding to a selected shape of the moon
The homeless seize discarded paper and cardboard
The working poor middle class gather round the table for Sunday dinner

The rich set there estate alarms and park their Bentleys

The softening of the wind lulls a cancer patient to sleep
While the darkening of light brings out the demons
Children tucked tight with forehead kisses
While across the street they hide under beds and in closets
Candles flicker upon stained glass and oak pews
Siren screams echo throughout the careless
Carefree city lights
And she beats off her attacker while walking home
A drunk driver takes a father from his family
While a new baby is born
New love is found
And a missing person is missed
In a moment
In one shared grain of hourglass sand
Worlds collide

SPLINTERED CROSSES

And the darkening dims
And the tired night drifts away
Into the solar break of day

SPLINTERED CROSSES

The 200

Two hundred babies
Slain by a jealous heart
The sin of Herod
The devil did impart

The blood of two and unders
Stained the Jewish land
Just because Herod found out
That he was not the man

A baby born King of the Jews
An unheard of claim to fame
But something sparked his jealous heart
To lay upon innocents his jealous blame

Israel's mother lay silent till now
Rachel wails from beyond the grave
Her cry of mourning ringing out
Even now in the churches nave

Take no chances was the plan
To save his unearned seat as king
Two hundred martyred but not dammed
Together on Rachael's lap they sing

The first two hundred so easily forgotten
But let us all remember and bow
The price for truth shall not be trodden
Christ the King now wears the crown

SPLINTERED CROSSES

Faith

A belief in the unseen
Is a part of all who see
Even though you cannot touch
It touches you just as much
With the soul, we see unseen
A world that lies in between
Even though we cannot touch
It touches us just as much

SPLINTERED CROSSES

I Think About You

Today I just want to think about you
Put away the world and its troubles too
To concentrate on home where I belong
To lose myself alone within the throng
I think about you all the time you know
Wherever I am wherever I go
I think about how I was when we met
At the sound of your voice my heart was rent
The things I loved in this life left me
Always wanting while lonely and empty
I think about the moment that you died
And the pardon for me your death provides
I think about you when I wake and sleep
I think about you when I laugh and weep

The Ghetto

I decided
I'd take a drive
to the part of town they call
the wrong side
where the humble poor live
in unison and community
Wall to wall loudness
of multicolored shiny paints
A lower south side forgotten
Forgotten by the better off
and well to do
Who believe they've made it
But in truth they're missing out
Rough roads to drive on
and lives to live
Yet a normalcy of mundane happiness
Hit and miss graffiti
And everything is for sale shops
With cars on their last legs
complete with unmatched tires
and exhaust leaks
A chunky boy about ten years old
holding the hand
of his kindergarten sister
Kids running around
Moms and dads on front porches
Watching
I blend in well in my well beaten civic
And dirty mechanic attire

SPLINTERED CROSSES

Heartaches are present
but, not on sleeved heart's
Only on the hand me down clothes
and new Nike 's
And all at once
The pretty picture in my head
Of where Jesus could be found
Fade
And the clear obviousness of the truth
fills my new seeing eyes
This is where he would come
This is where he would hang out
Mingle
Interact
Eat
Pray
This is where disciples would hang
on his every word
This is where he would come to speak

SPLINTERED CROSSES

Jury Duty

The quiet little city welcomes me
with the morning sunshine shining and bird songs chirped
and I make my way to the awaiting courthouse

As of yet I do not know why I'm here
in a line with I assume other law abiding citizens
to be chosen or cleared of service

We all stood silently round
a room wrapped in paneling of brown
And carpet blue on the ground
and mauve was on every chair

I felt like I was in church
they even had some pews
And the judge began to ask
reasons why he should let us pass
Or at least for certain days be excused

As I listened I began to think
about the kaleidoscope world
full of different lives operating in perfect sync

Vacation days and school starting
doctors appointment and families parting
one man has a son with Hodgkin's lymphoma starting chemotherapy
made my reasons seem a bit unfair and cheap

We exited the courthouse
for the street we all head
but I choose the sidewalk
so I don't end up dead
We all make our way back to our little lives
A deputy watches an inmate mow
jumpsuit of orange glow
And I think to myself that wasn't as bad
as I thought it would be

Just another small town day
of citizenship play

SPLINTERED CROSSES

Secluded Notes

I found seclusion
Between ear-budded headphones
They took me to a place of calming drift
Poetry in motion as if a train ride away
Escape momentarily into a small piece
Of peace

Eyes close soft and light
While ears absorb the vibes and rhymes
My heart beats within the rhythm
Synchronized with each drum beat
Eye twitches go to steady dark stare

The black and whites come in slow
Cascading tones of finger trickle
Over the ebony and ivory keys of soul elsewhere
And I am caught up into the third heaven
Consciousness of where am I
Is eclipsed by acoustic reverberations

Like seasonings on sustenance
A salting of steel chords begins mixing
The multitude of coursing sounds Rescue me
Not out of body but out of world
I am present but not wholly here

For the duration of the piece
I am taken away from silence and sound
For all there is, is the music

SPLINTERED CROSSES

Strums, beats and taps massage my thoughts
And for a moment
I am one with the vibrations

I am the bass drums hollow holler
I am the pickups of electrified six strings
I am the blending of the piano keys
I am become the music

SPLINTERED CROSSES

Where Were You?

Circulating wind in circular blow
Masters voice comes high to low
Calling out mortal questioner
Sound of woe
Stand up and man up
Tell me your name
Not that I don't know you
But that you hide not in your shame

Identify yourself, creation of mine
Who darkens the council
Advise sublime
With slack handed knowledge
You are far behind
Bend your ear and listen
For I will ask you this time
And you give the answers
To this my holy rhyme...

Was your existence present
Were you anywhere near
When I, yes I
Made the earth appear
When I, yes I
Laid the foundation and limit

Tell me O man
Do you understand

SPLINTERED CROSSES

Do you comprehend
Is your wisdom able to rend

Who decided its size
How big or small it should be
Who has the dimensions memorized
Who knows, surely it is thee

And tell me
To what is its foundation fastened
Can you even see

And who laid the first stone
There in the first corner
Who alone
Is this cutting of stone former

Did the angelic hosts of heaven
All the morning stars
Sing in unison
Were they close
Or were they far
When all the sons of God
Shouted for joy
With praise and exaltation
Where were you boy

Who shut the doors on the sea
To keep it at only so much
As it gushed from the womb beneath

SPLINTERED CROSSES

And I clothed it in clouds and hold it by the miry sludge

When my limit I fixed upon it
My bars and doors close it in
And I told it this is your limit
Your proud waves cannot extend

To be continued...

SPLINTERED CROSSES

The Silver Kiss.

Thirty silver pieces
A sinners ransom indeed
Someone to lead us right to him
Is all that we need

Enter Judas

One of the twelve
Bring him here to talk to me
I know for thirty he will help
For thirty, will he deceive

Judas, my fellow Jew
Have I got a deal for you
I have thirty pieces of silver here
You can have in exchange for your king

Satan was close by right then
Judas's heart he did enter in
In his ear he did speak
A perfect plan of deceit

Within his mouth a hollow hiss
It's sssssso ssssimple Judassssss
Just betray him with a kisssssss

Called a friend by his king
No longer meant anything
Satan's plan was in him now

SPLINTERED CROSSES

Betrayals infection the heart did plow

That night at supper the king did speak
Of how he knew of a coming deceit
The hushful room quietly still
And then with questions they began they to drill

Who is it lord?
Asked Peter and John
Who among us does not belong?

The dipper of the bread with me is he
The betrayer within
But let him be.

As they watched in disbelief
And all befallen with grief

The king turned his head
And to betrayer he said
Do what you've come to do

Betrayer's exit raised many a brow
As they wondered
What's he up to now?
Maybe he's going to buy more eats
Or maybe
He's the one sleeping with deceit

Later that night low in moonlight
The noise of the incoming guard

SPLINTERED CROSSES

And there at the lead
Satan's now full grown seed
Led them right up to the king

He told them
He who I kiss
Is the one that you wish
As the light from the torches lit that place

And there on kings face
Judas kissed away grace
And thus the silver kiss of betrayal
Was placed.

SPLINTERED CROSSES

The Keepers.

I am My Brother's Keeper
I will not waver from his side
I will not hide
We shall prop our arms upon our shoulders
Be my brother's holder
Onward trekking yonder skinny path
No easy task
Behold we climb
Combined
Together we weather
With hearts at tether
Onward marchward on
Move your feet
No retreat
Dirty footed soldiers
Brother's keepers to be kept
I will carry you to the roof
And lower you into the arms
Of truth beget
He is there
Don't fret
He is with us
For He too is His brother's keeper
And though we walk clean in dirty valley ground
I will wash thine feet bowed down
My basin is full
Come let me wash
Be still the dirt I've found
Do not cry

SPLINTERED CROSSES

You are again clean
On me thou lean
Come now soldier
Let us be going
The sun is setting
Time bestowing
Pilgrim's Progress
You and I
The pit of despond
Up to thine thigh
Hold my hand
Come on man
I see it now
The holy land
Be gone worldly wise men
And away with the pliable
Onward yon faithful
Strive towards the goal

SPLINTERED CROSSES

Limbo

I am lost in a realm of limbo, with tangibly illogical touch
A symphony to the eye in crescendo, seeing what we despise so much
Where am I, and why?
Where for art thou O my soul?
Have you strayed in the swamp you wade?
If only you would look up once more
Your feet would lose from the bog
And free trek you would once more
I understand you ditching our flesh
But in my continence alone, I die
Be brave, look up, we will be remembered
We will be redeemed
The planner has planned with his hands
We are more than just man
More than fearful sorrows
O my soul, don't stay so low solo in limbo
But rejoice in salvation's voice
The sound of sound and shine of shine
Come back, stay gone no longer

Anger.

Water in pot on stove of flame.
Slow heat torch beneath acclaim
Expansion of blood vessels, frying of nerves
Scorching of mind, simmering words
Stubbing of toe in dark of night
Finger poke in chest asking plight
Too much coffee and its hot outside
Bumper to bumper stopped traffic car ride
Bubbles start to form in the bottom of the pot
Flame turned up, add a little more hot
Molecules start to wiggle a bit
Evaporation starts stage one tantric fit
Liquid into gas
Molecules start moving fast
As water and heat do toil
And separation starts to boil
Blood pressure pounds skyward
Higher and higher loss of sanity byword
Raging pulse banging heart
Out of order alphabet with no end or start
Water to vapor steam burns thoughts
Rationality gone, patience shot
Like an engine at full throttle, over revved
I don't want to be like this, rather be dead
Boiling point reached
Now I must decide
Be angry and do not sin
Turn off the flame, let the heat reside
Or reach out in blinded fury

SPLINTERED CROSSES

Family sees you, begin to worry
Will he hurt us, will he lose his mind
Will he snap and maybe hurt us this time
Run hide, get away fast
Oh my God when will this pass.

SPLINTERED CROSSES

Borrowed Time

Spinning hands
Falling sand
The grandest plague
Of every man

No pause nor stopping
It marches on
It cannot be bought
Nor prolonged

You cannot touch It
It can't be seen
It cannot be reckoned with
Except in dreams

It's soft and quiet
Without hate or love
It is a curse and blessing
Ordained from above

We see its effects
On all mankind
And we believe it to be real
This thing called time

And though we see
Christ's effects on the world
We believe not
In his truth unfurled

SPLINTERED CROSSES

He holds each clock
Within his hand
And controls every falling
Of every grain of sand

We're all living
On borrowed time
And for this truth
I write this rhyme

SPLINTERED CROSSES

Christian Depression.

At the first
New
New sight
New vision
New heart
New man

Color's brighter
Warm warmer
Cold colder
Love freer
Life grander

Grace was fresh
Like the first day of spring
Like never before clean
Like hot summers day eating ice cream

I saw you everywhere
In everything
In everyone
I saw all the in betweens

I was high
I could fly
No good bye
Didn't care why

Absorbing all I could

All was good
No bad in sight
All day, no night

And then
All of the sudden
Dark grief
Infiltration thief

Heart grew heavy
Tears over levy
What have I done
What have I done

Then the comeback came
The cussing
The lusting
The Constant Untrusting

Walk by faith
turned in to
Hate my face
Hate that you had to die for my disgrace

I daily die in my unworthiness
Utterly disgusted with my unrighteousness
I know I can't pay you back
But
I want to be good

I hate sin with an almost

SPLINTERED CROSSES

unbridled passion
I barely maintain
As my heart goes insane

Now I'm trying to figure it all out
What does it mean
What do I do now
What's the purpose of this scene

It feels all alone
Like I'm waiting by the phone
But it don't ring
I can't hear, my heart no longer sings

What does it mean?

I love the church
But don't care to go
Like we're all plastic Christian's
Just putting on a show

I love the preaching
But the preachers just tell me to be better
No realistic teaching
No instructions how to get there

Oh what does it mean?
Please come back
Like you were at the beginning
Let me not fall through the cracks

SPLINTERED CROSSES

David Brian Hall
Dedication:

I would like to take a moment
and thank the Lord Jesus Christ
for saving my soul
and forgiving my sins
when I trip up.

I would also like to thank:
Sharie, my wife and inspiration, also our awesome kids
My mom, Brenda who asked me to do this project.
My dad, Ron Hall a wonderful and passionate preacher/pastor/missionary
who blessed this book with a few of his poetic pieces.
My grandparents,

SPLINTERED CROSSES

"Cric" & Ida
"Toots" & Joyce
My two sisters and tormentors Gina and Christy
An always supporting Aunt Norma
and one special supporter Rita
I thank all of these people
for their constant and special support.
A group of kind, loving country folks.

I would also like to take a moment
for
Travis
...

Down to the Garden

Back when creed road was paved with dirt
I'd go to visit Pa when I was just a little squirt
What a joy to walk through that kitchen door
Have Pa squeeze ya against those overalls once more

To everyone, Pa was an honest and true friend
Always ready to take a walk down to the garden
Now no, my Pa couldn't run around and play
But there was wisdom in what he had to say

Arthritis had long ago infected his hips
And tobacco stains were usually on his lips
He had to walk using an old wooden cane
And sometimes even that was too much pain

There was always love in those twinkling blue eyes
We'd go down to the garden under those Carolina skies
There was more to it than showing me taters and corn
These were vehicles upon which his wisdom was borne

I was just a kid and gardens didn't mean much to me
But now, oh how I wished I'd listened more intently

SPLINTERED CROSSES

Now you don't know how much memories means
If I could sit with Pa stringing another bucket of beans

To walk in to the aroma of pone bread in the air
Pintos and fatback now that's good eating there
Sometimes off driving to the store we'd go
For nothing else but to be friendly and say hello

All these precious memories are all so good
Sometimes love is not spoken it is just understood
These memories are mine but I alone cannot claim them
They belong to all who had the privilege to know him

A little while ago Pa got dressed in his finest overalls
And humbly went to answer the Lord's final call
The crowd was numerous that gathered around that day
Paying respects to a man that touched them all some way

Somewhere behind one of those mansions in the sky
A man is tending a garden, a man with a twinkle in his eye
The sunlight shining down, the maters nice red and round
The birds filling the springtime air with their sound

SPLINTERED CROSSES

The beans and corn all nice and neat in a row
Off walking he'll go just to be friendly and say hello
Did I mention that now there is no more pain
Or that he has finally ditched that old wooden cane

There's still love in those twinkling blue eyes
He invites you down to his garden under heavenly skies
He'll tell you, he's waiting for paradise to be complete
He's waiting by Jordan for his earthly bride to meet

He'll tell you that their earthly time was just the start
And that their time apart really breaks his heart
He knows that an earthly death is not the end
He is just waiting for her so eternity can truly begin

SPLINTERED CROSSES

Easter Sunday

It is a quite Sunday morning in a little southern town
We are all getting dressed up in our finest hand me downs
A glorious morning, the unofficial entrance of spring
Off in the distance I can hear those church bells ring
It is Easter Sunday and we'll have dinner on the grounds
The preacher will be smiling and shaking hands all around
The kids will be playing and showing off their new toys
The girls will be laughing and flirting with the boys
The birds are singing as I'm combing my unruly hair
I can almost hear the voices of that old gospel choir
The basses will be hitting the notes way down low
And each alto will be showing how high she can go
The kids will join in and sing as loud as they can
While the congregation smiles and claps their hands
Keeping time with the tunes and tuning out the time
Listening and loving some good old gospel rhyme

Preacher will preach what the good Lord has given
And with fire and thunder each point will be driven
There'll be an altar call and each Christian will pray
That any lost sinner will find the heavenly way
The gift of salvation is free and given to us all
Just open up your heart and answer His sweet call
…
It is Easter Sunday and everybody has come
To worship the resurrection of God's only Son

SPLINTERED CROSSES

Church Bells

Yon church bells do gloriously sound
Sending their message to all around
The doors are open, it's time to begin
Welcome are all, who will enter in

Yon church bells do merrily chime
Calling two singles one last time
The sun warmly shines on this day
A beaming couple they drive away

Yon church bells do excitedly ring
A newborn babe does heartily sing
Winds carry sounds of joy through the air
Proud joyous smiles abound everywhere

Yon church bells do gloomily toll
As death into happiness creepily stole
A child whose future seemed so bright
Faded to darkness, cries echo long into the night

Yon church bells do eternally strike
Its message we do not always like
Through happiness and joy, heartache and strife
Dutifully signaling a moment in the circle of life

Apple Pie

Oh the sweet smell of homemade apple pie
With a flaky brown crust that fills the eye
Like the ones Mrs. Payne cools on the windowsill
Just to sink my teeth in you would be a thrill

But if was to I snatch one warm juicy pie
Out from under her keen watchful eye
I am sure that she'd raise quite a ruckus
I would have to be extremely cautious

A slight breeze floats fresh aromas straight to me
I can't resist; I know I should turn and flee
Then the screen door opens and there she stands
Flour and dough still on her apron and hands

Looking around she places her hands on her hips
A faint weathered smile curls her knowing lips
She glances slowly at the golden leaves
Dancing their last dance in fall's gentle breeze

Then her voice as pretty and gentle as a song
Said "Hey there Billy, well now come along
I have something for more than your eye
A piece of freshly made, sweet apple pie"

Cascade

Cascade down on me
Blessings from above
Blessings gifted from
The One filled with love
Cascade down on me
Blessings like waterfalls of love

Fill me with your light
Hope and eternal wonder
Let me go out into the night
Reaching to the ones going under
Cascade down on me
A passion like roaring thunder

Cascade down on me
Blessings from above
Cascade down on me
Your strength and eternal love
Cascade down on me
Like a million turtledoves

Fill me with your desire
To reach out to the lost
To the uttermost
No matter the cost

Cascade down on me
Like tears from the cross
Cascade down on me
Your Love eternally

SPLINTERED CROSSES

These Shoes

With my blue eyes and wispy blond hair
I looked at these shoes, my first dress up pair
My mawmaw and pawpaw got them for me
They were laughing and smiling radiantly
My mommy would pick me out a frilly dress
And with these shoes I was ready to impress
Sunday morning it was go to church day
With my new shoes all eyes would turn my way
Everyone with smiles they couldn't hide
Mawmaw and Pawpaw beaming with pride
And they did, I know, because I saw
Thank you mawmaw, thank you pawpaw

Now I would like to give them back to you
I know you can't wear them, I wouldn't ask you to
But please just keep them somewhere lying around
And sometimes on gloomy days when you are down
And something bad has given you the blues
Go and pull out this pair of black dress shoes
Take a moment or two and give them a shine
And enjoy a little trip back to another time
Remember the joy on this Christmas day
Know my heart will never be very far away

SPLINTERED CROSSES

Prayer Room Warriors

The Faithful Ones
Bend a prayerful knee
To send up for others
A merciful plea

Steady year after year
They pray constantly
Shed honest tear after tear
In earnest for you and me

These Faithful Ones
Are in high demand
Who by kneeling down
They take a stand

The Prayer

Why, why pray now?
It's just a Christmas snack
I didn't really want to wait
I was hungry ready to attack

With my closed mind
Like the Pharisee
I had become blind
I could not see

She solemnly bowed her head
Slowly the words began to come out
Honest word by pure word
Sincere and earnest without a doubt

She thanked the Lord for all the food
She thanked the Lord for the happy day
Thanked Him for the people gathered there
And for all His blessings along the way

The room became solemnly quiet and still
The Holy One joined us in the room there
Linking us all together in that moment
A moment bound by a dear saint's prayer

She prayed in earnest for one and another
She prayed for the dear solder's overseas
Prayed for all the poor ones suffering loss
Tears flowed silently at her heartfelt pleas

SPLINTERED CROSSES

Many prayers went to the heavenly skies
By the time her precious prayer was done
Happy tears were wiped from many eyes
Praise and glory to the Father and the Son

I went expecting something to eat
And I can definitely say that I got fed
I must humble myself and repent
And more often by the Spirit be led

SPLINTERED CROSSES

A Steady Even Flow

I remember your patience, your steady even flow
Here is something that I want you to know
When I became a daddy I wanted to be just like you
For I remembered all the things that we would do

Hands that showed me how to catch a softly thrown ball
The love in your eyes as you picked me up from a fall
Arms that demonstrated easy graceful baseball swings
These memories are some of my most precious things

You knew what I needed and just how much it took
The words that you would read from the good book
Telling me about a hell below and a heaven above
And yes, chastisement administered out of love

The pride in your eyes when I made the team
They had never shone brighter or so it seemed
Even when I did not play and I just rode the pine
I remember the togetherness what a special time

But now I finally realize we are different yet the same

What before I could not see, now slowly grows plain
You've connected me to a power source for whatever I do
I've learned to trust in the same God that saw you though

But your smiling eyes tell me that this, you already know
An understanding that comes from a steady even flow

SPLINTERED CROSSES

A Working Man

Machines with their perpetual grind
Forklifts race around with a hearty whine
Big little chiefs parade around
Jotting every little detail down
Another useless mark in another book
A working man toils alone high in a nook
He is working on some exhaust fans
With stains on shirt and grease on his hands
He wipes his sweaty brow with his sleeve
As an answered prayer brings a slight breeze
He doesn't need a downward glance
To know if he falls he hasn't a chance
Pausing to wipe sweat before it reaches his eye
He works on at over a fifty feet high
Flip the power switch and wait to see
The blades start to turn rhythmically
He climbs down rung by rung
Satisfied the job is finally done

Mayberry, My City, Mayberry

Mayberry, Mayberry, my charming rustic city
Lived in by few, but claimed and loved by many
Among these streets thousands of strangers roam
Strangers completely comfortable, almost at home

Built on the back of farmers in their Red-Camel coveralls
Work boots covered in red mud, driving their Farm Alls
Laid back never dreaming they'd become history
All because of one boy's dreams, a boy named Andy

Andy Griffith's show became famous, as did our city
Now we have a committee to keep it nice and pretty
For all those curious tourists that comes busing in
While those farmers just shake their heads and grin

Seems there are not as many tobacco barns anymore
Some of them have been turned into old country stores
Now we are about growing grapes and making wines
The tobacco plant has been replaced by Vidal vines

SPLINTERED CROSSES

During the annual fall festival of the Autumn Leaves
Artisans line the streets that are packed thick as thieves
We have the Mayberry Days and many other events for all
Old men argue politics and young men brag about football

Donna Fargo was a huge country star, we claim her too
We named an entire highway after her just to remind you
The Easter Brothers and their gifts to gospel music industry
Don't forget about the largest open faced granite quarry

For me the best thing about Mayberry, my beautiful city
It is the goodness of these people, plainly and simply
Good old country people, truly the salt of the earth
Coming together over and over to prove their worth

There may be a few famous people that put us on the map
But most souls pulled themselves up by their bootstrap

SPLINTERED CROSSES

At the end of the day when the tourist buses pull away
It's just another country evening just like every other day

But there's a whole lot more here than meets the eye
Some waters run much deeper than tourist dollars can buy
The last war we had here tore families' apart, Blue vs Grey
On Main St. there's a memorial to our boys that passed away

Praying for peace and safety on bended knees we toil
As needlessly our soldier's blood runs red on foreign soil
Since WW1 and ever since, every time a casket comes home
A city grieves as another familiar name gets etched in stone

SPLINTERED CROSSES

Back Porch Rocking Chairs

When we are old and it is time for us to rest
We will sit in our rocking chairs outside our nest

Patiently, lovingly we will just quietly rock on
We will listen to the whisper of the winds gentle song

We will sit and enjoy the beauty of the Carolina skies
Tangerine sunsets that we will watch with satisfied eyes

Grandchildren run and laugh barefoot through the grasses
Sunlight glistens off sweet tea poured in Mason jar glasses

Hand in hand for our many blessings we give thanks
Including old rocking chairs creaking over wooden planks

When our time has come and we are dead and gone
And our chairs rock on the porch empty and alone

Don't mourn or cry for us dear family and friends
Sit and hear our souls in the song of the whispering winds

SPLINTERED CROSSES

Broken Little Man

I never had a chance to be a normal little kid
Laughing and playing like all the other boys did
Cause from the start my daddy had a heavy hand
One day he finally broke this little man
Oh my Mama knew the damage he could do
It was worse when he had a drink or two
But she closed her eyes and turned away
I'll never forget that dreadful day
I lay there in a broken twisted heap
Too scared to move or even weep
Choking back a futile desperate cry
Silent tears streamed from my eyes
The doctors all agreed there was no hope
They said I had snapped like a brittle rope
Confined to a wheelchair and a lonely room
Deeply depressed and full of gloom
Daddy never came; mama came once this year
I don't believe anyone remembers that I'm here
Broken physically and mentally waiting to die
Anguish filled days slowly crawled by
Then one night a man appeared in my bedroom
Handed me a book, smiled and said I'll be back soon
It was a beautiful book; gold letters on shiny red
But how did that man just appear beside my bed?
I must have been asleep when he sneaked in
I looked at the book oddly anxious to begin
I read it slowly from cover to cover
A book so unique like no other

I began to read that book every day
It was a ray of light to show me the way
Didn't understand it all, but I read it just the same
I seemed to be drawn to it like a moth to a flame
Then one day a white-haired preacher came by
He was honest and he looked me in the eye
His eyes sparkled a crystal clear blue
He simply told me, Jesus loves you
And he told me the story of his Savior's love
How He sent His only Son down from above
He took out his bible and read me some words
It was like springtime and a chorus of birds
It was the same as my own little red book!
My whole body with excitement shook
Tell me! Show me! Teach me! I cried
Tell me why this Jesus man died
Tell me why some people hated him so
While others followed wherever he'd go
Simply, plainly the story did unfold
He led me from the manger down Roman's Road
To Golgotha's cross where I lost my sinner's load
There my transformation was complete
A miraculous cleansing so unique
I write this note laying on my deathbed
Awaiting a glorious reunion up ahead
I hope my note will be an inspiration
It was written with a prayerful dedication
Daddy never came; mama hasn't been in over a year
I don't believe any one will really miss me here
As I close my eyes and slip into eternity

SPLINTERED CROSSES

I beg you, don't feel sorry for me
I contemplate earthly to heavenly things
Like trading wheelchairs for wings
This bed and room I won't need anymore
I'm already knocking on Heaven's door

SPLINTERED CROSSES

If That Isn't Love

We waddle in our own small worlds full of self-pity
And think of our own burdens, alas and oh poor me
But what comes to my pondering mind
Is what transpired in another place and time

When a man climbed up a hill called Mount Calvary
Stretched forth willing arms and died upon a tree
I think of the crown of thorns that pierced his brow
That He wore thinking of you and me even now

Upon that cross, He bore the world's sins upon his breast
Imagine the cat o' nine tails, the pain too much to digest
Holy blood ran from jagged tears on his back and chest
Gasping for a breath of air, in ultimate agony, unable to rest

With love still in His eyes, his last breath was spent
Skies darkened, sun was hid, and the temple veil was rent
From being born in a simple stable manger of a lowly birth

Full of love and compassion He had walked upon this earth

Not caring about high places or a royal throne
Just a loving caring person, no home of His own
Living in truth, each and every lesson that He taught
Did He suffer the agony of the cross for naught?

Of the final redeeming blood, every drop was caught
To the heavenly Father, His own blood He brought
In spite of it all, he still died agonizingly slow
If that isn't love, then what is? I don't know

SPLINTERED CROSSES

I Can't Let Go

The death rattle is racking my failing lungs.
Soon my funeral songs will be softly sung.
Family members have all tearily come.
Around me, angels shine like the golden sun.

Oh how I long to let go of all this pain!
So much for me to see and so much to gain.
However, you see I cannot just let go.
For it is all of you, my children that I love so.

Above, friends and family patiently awaits.
Precious arms of Jesus are inside those pearly gates.
Thin white hair is matted to the side of my head.
Skeletal hands grasp the metal rails of this hospice bed.

My earthly beauty may have long been gone.
Pain racks this mortal body yet I still hang on.
My child, my child I just have to know.
Are you ready? Are you going to go?

Our Town (Mayberry)

We love everything about our little town
Where friendliness seems to abound
Visit the museum and stay for a while
You will leave with memories and a smile

Nestled in the foothills amid beautiful scenery
Always resplendent with fauna and greenery
The backbone of the community hard-working and strong
Always willing to work together and get along

Our history varied, unique and deep
From Mount Pilot to where the Siamese twins sleep
A haircut at Floyd's was sweeter than candy
Swing by and take a picture with Opie and Andy

Several generations grew up on the show
Yes, it's not real, a fact that we all know
You can't cut a tree with a butter knife
Can't deny the similarities to our way of life

Now Andy and Barney, well they aren't around
To bring their brand of law and order to our town
Andy has left it in good hands no doubt
Goodhearted citizens still on patrol throughout

Every guy wants a country gal on his arm
That was raised with Mayberry charm

SPLINTERED CROSSES

And he hopes that she can cook like Aunt Bee
If she's as pretty as Thelma Lou that's just fantasy!

Visit the world's largest open-faced granite quarry
Climb Mt. Pilot in all its open-aired glory
Read up about the life of the Siamese twins
Listen to the local storyteller spin his spins

Come visit our charming little town
So many exciting things to be found
Let this be the place to start
For your next adventure of the heart

SPLINTERED CROSSES

Judgment Day

"That's the third friend this year, how can I continue on?
This is Travis, my best friend, my cousin he can't be gone"
Through the anguishing hours of blackened night
Into the wee waning hours of dawn's early light

The frozen chill of death has blanketed our home
I stare blankly at the pages of God's heavy tome
Death's merciless hammer has crashed my heart
Millions of razor edged shards have ripped it apart

Left me with burning tears streaming from my eyes
"WHY GOD" I scream in anguish into the skies
My finite mind struggles with the right and wrong
As I rant and rave against death's haunting song

"He was too young to go and had so many reasons to stay
Yet sorrowfully it seems to always end this blasted way"
Tomorrow, I must say my last earthly goodbyes
Comfort others while choking back my own cries

"Dear Jesus please give Travis a good place to stay
Show him where Pa and Grandma lives along the way"

SPLINTERED CROSSES

I can see them smiling and rising to welcome him home
Knowing he's in such good hands helps me carry on

"Lord, I know you stand at the door and knock"
In this day and time we all should take stock
I am here on bended knee to repent and pray
So my heart is pure and ready on judgment day"

SPLINTERED CROSSES

The River

In the charming Carolina foothills
It flows steadily, yet tranquil and still
Morning mountain showers fuel it along
To all so picturesque wide and strong

Between right or wrong it can't hope to tell
Sometimes its called to ring death's gloomy bell
Old Man River sings a tune to death's chime
Pain of a soul taken before its time

Too late a body is pulled from the deep
Peacefully rested in heavenly sleep
Mossy rocks channel a gradual descent
Nature hums a gentle empty lament

Meandering among the weeping trees
Saffron rays glisten on whispering leaves

What Does It Take?

What does it take to teach the world about salvation?
With the omnipresent God as your foundation
The boundaries of this world are so small
What else do you need to answer the call?

FAITH ... To put aside the doubts and fears
To turn away from doubters with deaf ears
To put aside all personal emotion
To pack it all up and cross the ocean

DEVOTION ... To follow God no matter what the cost
Not worrying about or counting what is gained or lost
Except the souls in the jungle or on the mountain
Depending on Him as guide, strength, eternal fountain

COURAGE ... To endure the danger, toils and strife
To accomplish what God has called you to do in your life
Not for any worldly fame, fortune or recognition
But to teach the lost God's simple plan of salvation

LOVE ... To put God first in your lives
With sad farewells and teary goodbyes
Leaving all church, family and friends

SPLINTERED CROSSES

Just one soul makes it worthwhile in the end

We can never know what all you've given
But we thank you for teaching us about living
We can never know what all it took
But we thank you for teaching us the book
We can never know what all you have done
But we can thank you for teaching us about the son

Without the qualities that you taught
Or lessons learned and battles fought
We don't know where we would be today
But we know tomorrow how to find the way

SPLINTERED CROSSES

Forevermore

Hours burn and the owl takes flight
Yet my hands still yearn to write
This moment may come and go
But He is always, this I now know

Sheep will bleat and the lion will roar
Fish will swim and the eagle will soar
If they all die out and are no more
Yet He will still reign forevermore

Our heavens and earth may pass away
Lives are but a moment in my Lord's Day
So leave your memories of me in the past
For in my new role for Him I am cast

Lessons learned out on the mission field
He takes care of all who to Him do yield
Praying always on from bended knees
Prayer winds whisper through the trees

We learn from the people in our life
We learn to walk together without strife
Learn from all the love, pain, gain and loss
Most of all, the One who died on the cross

All men and women's lives can bloom
If their past under the blood they entomb
Their lives can be reborn under grace
Unburdened and free to run His race

SPLINTERED CROSSES

Lifeline

Never knowing what it truly means
To sail my ship and chase my dreams
My tortured life full of dark secret lies
Chasing hope beyond foreign skies

A perpetual season of discontent
Chasing sails from York to the Orient
My life appeared normal but mundane
Inside I was raging and going insane

Constant waves and endless horizons
Bastions on cliffs sending beacons
Lost and adrift on life's endless sea
Would anybody throw a lifeline to me?

My ever-present smile was a mask
Cracking jokes to hide was my task
Into a silver flask I try to drown
My endless sorrows eddy down

Toss the flask and grab the rail
To the heavens I plead and wail
"God in heaven, are you out there?"
A lifeline came in answer to my prayer

Now a family united sits in a pew
Father, I give all the glory to you

Love

under
guiding
star
a Son
born
Bethlehem stable to Place of the Skulls
hay filled manger to splintered cross
Love pouring out
through acts
teaching
miracles
Love
flowing
deeper than
shed blood

www.ingramcontent.com/pod-product-compliance
Lightning Source LLC
Chambersburg PA
CBHW031404040426
42444CB00005B/407